THE BOOK
OF
- TERRIBLY AWESOME -

DAD JOKES

Dan Gilden

I TRIED TO ORGANIZE A PROFESSIONAL HIDE AND SEEK TOURNAMENT, BUT IT WAS A COMPLETE FAILURE.

GOOD PLAYERS ARE HARD TO FIND.

MY DAUGHTER THINKS I DON'T GIVE HER ENOUGH PRIVACY.

AT LEAST THAT'S WHAT SHE SAID IN HER DIARY.

WHAT DID BEETHOVEN BECOME AFTER HE DIED?

A DECOMPOSER.

GOOD ROMANCE STARTS WITH GOOD FRIENDSHIP.

A BAD ROMANCE STARTS WITH "RA RA AH AH AH. RO, RO MA MA GA GA, OOH LA LA,"

WHAT DID THE PIRATE SAY ON HIS 80TH BIRTHDAY?

"AYE MATEY!"

DOES ANYONE KNOW HOW TO CHARGE MILK?

BECAUSE MINE IS STUCK AT 1%

WHY DO SCUBA DIVERS FALL BACKWARD INTO THE WATER?

BECAUSE IF THEY FELL FORWARD, THEY'D STILL BE IN THE BOAT.

WHAT DO YOU CALL A SNOBBISH CRIMINAL WALKING DOWN THE STAIRS?

A CON-DESCENDING.

A BOSSY MAN GOES INTO A BAR.

HE ORDERS EVERYONE A ROUND.

SOMEONE STOLE THE TOILET SEAT AT THE POLICE STATION.

INVESTIGATORS HAVE NOTHING TO GO ON.

IF I GOT 50 CENTS FOR EVERY FAILED MATH EXAM,

I'D HAVE $ 7.20 NOW.

WHAT CONCERT CAN YOU VISIT FOR 45 CENTS?

50 CENT PLUS NICKELBACK.

WHAT'S ATHEISM?

IT'S A NON-PROPHET ORGANIZATION.

EBAY IS SO USELESS.

I TRIED TO LOOK UP LIGHTERS AND ALL THEY
HAD WAS 12,735 MATCHES.

WHENEVER A BIG BUG HIT THE WINDSHIELD AND LEFT A MARK MY DAD WOULD SAY,

"IT SURE TOOK A LOT OF GUTS TO DO THAT."

DAD: "HEY, SON. WHAT ARE YOU DRINKING?"

SON: "SOY MILK."

DAD: "HOLA, MILK. SOY PADRE."

WHY WAS 6 AFRAID OF 7?

BECAUSE 7 WAS A REGISTERED SIX OFFENDER.

WHY DIDN'T THE TOILET PAPER MAKE IT ACROSS THE ROAD?

HE MET WITH TOO MANY CRACKS ON THE WAY.

WHY CAN'T YOU HEAR A PTERODACTYL GO TO THE BATHROOM?

BECAUSE THE PEE IS SILENT.

MY FATHER HAS THE HEART OF A LION...

AND A LIFETIME BAN FROM THE NATIONAL ZOO.

HOW MANY TICKLES DOES IT TAKE TO MAKE AN OCTOPUS LAUGH?

TEN-TICKLES.

WHAT DO YOU CALL AN EMPTY CAN OF CHEESE WHIZ?

CHEESE WAS!

A FURNITURE STORE KEEPS CALLING ME.

ALL I WANTED WAS ONE NIGHT STAND.

THIEVES HAD BROKEN INTO MY HOUSE AND STOLEN EVERYTHING EXCEPT MY TOWELS, SOAP, SHOWER GEL, AND MY DEODORANT.

DIRTY BASTARDS.

DID YOU HEAR ABOUT THE GUY WHO HAD THE WHOLE LEFT SIDE OF HIS BODY AMPUTATED?

YEAH, HE'S ALRIGHT NOW.

"DID YOU TAKE A SHOWER TODAY?"

"SURE, DAD."

"WELL, YOU BETTER RETURN IT!"

TO THE MAN IN THE WHEELCHAIR WHO STOLE MY CAMOUFLAGE JACKET...

YOU CAN HIDE BUT YOU CAN'T RUN!

I NEVER WANTED TO BELIEVE MY DAD WAS STEALING FROM HIS JOB AS A ROAD WORKER.

BUT WHEN I GOT HOME, ALL THE SIGNS WERE THERE.

WHAT HAPPENED ON THE 1.1.1111?

A NEW YEAR STARTED.

FIVE GUYS WALK INTO A BAR.

YOU THINK ONE OF THEM WOULD'VE SEEN IT.

MY WIFE IS ALWAYS TELLING ME WHAT TO DO BUT WHEN SHE TOLD ME TO STOP BEING A FLAMINGO,

WELL, THAT'S WHEN I PUT MY FOOT DOWN!

WIFE TO HUSBAND: "I'M PREGNANT."

HUSBAND TO WIFE(TRYING TO BE FUNNY): "HI PREGNANT, I'M DAD."

WIFE: "NO, YOU'RE NOT."

HOW IS YOUR LONG-DISTANCE RELATIONSHIP GOING?

SO FAR, SO GOOD.

DON'T YOU HATE IT WHEN PEOPLE ANSWER THEIR OWN QUESTIONS? I DO.

THANKS FOR EXPLAINING THE WORD "MANY" TO ME,

IT MEANS A LOT.

WHY DID THE SHOW ABOUT PLANES NEVER TAKE OFF?

IT HAD A LOUSY PILOT.

WHOEVER INVENTED KNOCK-KNOCK JOKES

DESERVES A NO-BELL PRIZE.

WHAT IS BLACK, COOL, AND STANDS IN A FOREST?

A DEER IN A LEATHER JACKET.

I HAD A PRIEST PERFORM AN EXORCISM FOR MY HOUSE, BUT I NEVER PAID THE BILL...

IT'S BEEN REPOSSESSED.

MY THERAPIST TOLD ME TO WRITE LETTERS TO PEOPLE I HATED AND THEN BURN THEM.

I'VE DONE THAT, BUT WHAT DO I DO WITH THE LETTER?

WHY DO COWS WEAR BELLS?

BECAUSE THEIR HORNS DON'T WORK!

WHY DON'T ANTS GET SICK?

BECAUSE THEY HAVE LITTLE ANTIBODIES.

WHAT DO AN APPLE AND AN ORANGE HAVE IN COMMON?

NEITHER ONE CAN DRIVE.

WHAT IS BLACK AND WHITE AND READ ALL OVER?

TWO NUNS IN A CHAINSAW FIGHT!

WHAT DID GEORGE WASHINGTON SAY TO HIS MEN BEFORE THEY CROSSED THE DELAWARE?

GET IN THE BOAT.

I JUST WATCHED A DOCUMENTARY ABOUT BEAVERS.

IT WAS THE BEST DAM SHOW I EVER SAW!

WHAT IS THE WORST COMBINATION OF TWO
SICKNESSES?

DIARRHEA AND ALZHEIMER'S. YOU'RE RUNNING,
BUT YOU DON'T KNOW WHERE.

WHAT IS THE DIFFERENCE BETWEEN
IGNORANCE AND APATHY?

I DON'T KNOW, AND I DON'T CARE.

WHAT IS THE DIFFERENCE BETWEEN PEOPLE FROM ABU DHABI AND FROM DUBAI?

THE PEOPLE FROM DUBAI DON'T LIKE THE FLINTSTONES, BUT THE PEOPLE FROM ABU DHABI DOOOOOOOO!

IF YOU ARE RUSSIAN WHEN HEADED TO THE BATHROOM AND FINNISH WHEN YOU COME OUT, WHAT ARE YOU WHEN YOU ARE IN THE BATHROOM?

EUROPEAN

HAVE YOU EVER TRIED TO EAT A CLOCK?

IT'S VERY TIME-CONSUMING.

YOU KNOW WHY THE OLD LADY FELL DOWN
THE WELL?

SHE DIDN'T SEE THAT WELL.

WHY ARE ELEVATOR JOKES SO CLASSIC AND GOOD?

THEY WORK ON MANY LEVELS.

HAVE YOU HEARD ABOUT THE DYSLEXIC DEVIL WORSHIPPER?

HE SOLD HIS SOUL TO SANTA.

I'VE RECENTLY DISCOVERED I'M TERRIFIED OF ELEVATORS,

SO I'M TAKING STEPS TO AVOID THEM.

I WAS A LITTLE AFRAID OF SPEED BUMPS TOO,

BUT I'M SLOWLY GETTING OVER THEM!

I CAN'T BELIEVE PEOPLE ARE STILL MAKING "FRIENDS" REFERENCES 15 YEARS AFTER THE SHOW ENDED.

NO ONE TOLD ME LIFE WAS GONNA BE THIS WAY.

THE FIRST COMPUTER DATES BACK TO ADAM AND EVE.

IT WAS AN APPLE WITH LIMITED MEMORY, JUST ONE BYTE. AND THEN EVERYTHING CRASHED.

I STILL REMEMBER THE LAST THING MY GRANDFATHER SAID BEFORE KICKING THE BUCKET...

"HEY, YOU WANT TO SEE HOW FAR I CAN KICK THIS BUCKET?"

"DOCTOR, THERE'S A PATIENT ON LINE 1 THAT SAYS HE'S INVISIBLE"

"WELL, TELL HIM I CAN'T SEE HIM RIGHT NOW."

MY WIFE DUMPED ME THE OTHER DAY. SAID I DIDN'T LISTEN TO HER.

OR SOMETHING LIKE THAT.

WHAT DOES EVERY TICKLE ME ELMO GET BEFORE LEAVING THE FACTORY?

TWO TEST TICKLES.

WHY IS THERE A MUSIC FROM THE PRINTER?

MAYBE THE PAPER IS JAMMING.

WHAT'S THE DUMBEST ANIMAL IN THE JUNGLE?

A POLAR BEAR.

WHAT'S RED AND BAD FOR YOUR TEETH?

A BRICK.

WHAT IS THE DIFFERENCE BETWEEN A HIPPO AND A ZIPPO?

WELL, A HIPPO IS REALLY HEAVY, AND A ZIPPO IS JUST A LITTLE LIGHTER!

I DON'T TELL DAD JOKES OFTEN,

BUT WHEN I DO, HE LAUGHS.

ME: "I'M GOING TO GO CHANGE."

DAD (ALWAYS): "DON'T CHANGE! I LIKE YOU THE WAY YOU ARE!"

WHAT IS WHITE AND HIDES BEHIND A TREE?

A SHY MILK.

YOU KNOW WHAT OFTEN GETS OVERLOOKED?

GARDEN FENCES!

TWO WINDMILLS ARE STANDING IN A FIELD. ONE ASKS, "WHAT'S YOUR FAVORITE STYLE OF MUSIC?"

THE OTHER SAYS, "I'M A BIG METAL FAN."

OUTSIDE OF A DOG, A BOOK IS A MAN'S BEST FRIEND.

INSIDE OF A DOG... IT'S TOO DARK TO READ.

I REALLY WANT TO BUY ONE OF THOSE SUPERMARKET CHECKOUT DIVIDERS,

BUT THE LADY BEHIND THE TILL KEEPS PUTTING IT BACK.

IF PEOPLE STOOD SHOULDER TO SHOULDER AROUND THE EQUATOR...

2/3 OF THEM WOULD DROWN.

I'M NOT A BIG FAN OF STAIRS.

THEY'RE ALWAYS UP TO SOMETHING.

WHAT'S E. T. SHORT FOR?

BECAUSE HE'S ONLY GOT LITTLE LEGS!

DAD BUYS A UNIVERSAL REMOTE AND SAYS,

"THIS CHANGES EVERYTHING!"

WHEN DOES A JOKE BECOME A DAD JOKE?

WHEN THE PUNCHLINE IS APPARENT.

PLASTIC SURGERY USED TO BE SUCH A TABOO SUBJECT.

NOW YOU CAN TALK ABOUT BOTOX AND NOBODY RAISES AN EYEBROW.

WHAT'S THE DIFFERENCE BETWEEN AN ORAL AND A RECTAL THERMOMETER?

THE TASTE!

WHAT'S GERMAN FOR AN UNEXPECTED
PREGNANCY?

KINDER SURPRISE.

WHAT DID YODA SAY WHEN HE SAW HIMSELF
IN 4K?

HDMI

MY SON TIED HIS FIRST TIE TODAY. I LOOKED AT HIM AND TOLD HIM,

"KNOT BAD SON."

LANCE IS A PRETTY UNCOMMON NAME TODAY.

IN MEDIEVAL TIMES PEOPLE WERE NAMED LANCE A LOT.

DID YOU HEAR ABOUT THE CHAMELEON WHO COULDN'T CHANGE COLORS?

HE HAD A REPTILE DYSFUNCTION.

TWO GOLDFISH ARE IN A TANK. ONE LOOKS AT THE OTHER AND SAYS,

"I'LL MAN THE GUN, YOU STEER"

TWO GOLDFISH ARE IN A TANK. ONE LOOKS AT THE OTHER AND SAYS,

"DO YOU KNOW HOW TO DRIVE THIS THING?!"

TWO SOLDIERS ARE IN A TANK. ONE LOOKS AT THE OTHER AND SAYS,

"BLUBLUBBLUBLUBBLUB."

MY ADDICTION TO HELIUM IS OUT OF CONTROL...

BUT NO ONE TAKES MY CRIES FOR HELP SERIOUSLY.

A MAN TRIED TO SELL ME A COFFIN TODAY...

I TOLD HIM THAT'S THE LAST THING I NEED.

"DAD, DID YOU GET A HAIRCUT?"

"NO, I GOT THEM ALL CUT."

WHY DID THE COACH GO TO THE BANK?

TO GET HIS QUARTER BACK.

I LIKE TO SPEND EVERY DAY AS IF IT'S MY LAST.

STAYING IN BED AND CALLING FOR A NURSE TO BRING ME MY PUDDING.

DID YOU HEAR ABOUT THE TWO THIEVES WHO STOLE A CALENDAR?

THEY EACH GOT SIX MONTHS.

WIFE: "YOU REALLY HAVE NO SENSE OF DIRECTION, DO YOU?"

HUSBAND: "WHERE DID THAT COME FROM?"

MY DEAF GIRLFRIEND WAS TALKING IN HER SLEEP LAST NIGHT.

DAMN NEAR POKED MY EYE OUT.

I TRIED TO SUE THE AIRPORT FOR MISPLACING MY LUGGAGE.

I LOST MY CASE.

I WANTED TO LEARN HOW TO DRIVE A STICK SHIFT.

BUT I COULDN'T FIND A MANUAL.

I WAS SITTING IN TRAFFIC THE OTHER DAY...

PROBABLY WHY I GOT RUN OVER.

WHAT'S THE MOST TERRIFYING WORD IN NUCLEAR PHYSICS?

"OOPS!"

WHY DOES A SEAGULL FLY OVER THE SEA?

BECAUSE IF IT FLEW OVER THE BAY, IT'D BE A BAGEL!

MY DOG USED TO CHASE PEOPLE ON BIKES. IT GOT SO BAD,

I EVENTUALLY HAD TO TAKE HIS BIKES OFF HIM.

HOW DO YOU ORGANIZE A PARTY IN SPACE?

YOU PLANET.

WHAT'S AN ASTRONAUT'S FAVORITE PART OF A COMPUTER?

THE SPACE BAR.

I BROKE MY LEG IN TWO PLACES. AND YOU KNOW WHAT MY DOCTOR TOLD ME?

"STAY OUT OF THOSE PLACES!"

DID YOU KNOW THAT BIRTHDAYS ARE GOOD FOR YOUR HEALTH?

THE MORE YOU HAVE, THE LONGER YOU LIVE.

WHAT IS HAIRY, ROUND, AND BROWN AND GOES UP AND DOWN?

A KIWI IN AN ELEVATOR.

WHAT IS WHITE, STANDS IN FRONT OF THE STAIRS, AND CAN'T GO UP?

A WASHING MACHINE.

SOMEONE BROKE INTO MY HOUSE LAST NIGHT AND STOLE ALL MY ANTIDEPRESSANTS.

WELL, I HOPE THEY'RE HAPPY.

ONCE I WAS ABDUCTED BY A GROUP OF MIMES.

THEY DID UNSPEAKABLE THINGS TO ME.

I HAVE A VERY SECURE JOB.

THERE'S NOBODY ELSE WHO WOULD WANT IT.

I WANTED TO BE A DOCTOR...

BUT I DIDN'T HAVE THE PATIENTS.

ANYBODY CAN GET BURIED WHEN THEY DIE,
IF YOU WANT TO BE CREMATED...

YOU HAVE TO URN IT.

PEOPLE SAY THEY'RE WORRIED THAT MY
MAGICIAN FRIEND IS DOING HIS DISAPPEARING
ACT TOO OFTEN.

BUT I KNOW IT'S JUST A STAGE HE'S GOING
THROUGH.

WHAT HAPPENS IF YOU THROW A GREEN
ROCK INTO THE RED SEA?

IT GETS WET.

WHAT WOULD THE TERMINATOR BE CALLED IN
HIS RETIREMENT?

THE EXTERMINATOR.

A DAD WAS WASHING THE CAR WITH HIS SON.

SON: "DAD, COULD YOU PLEASE USE A SPONGE?"

DID YOU KNOW THAT DIARRHEA IS HEREDITARY?

IT RUNS IN YOUR JEANS.

IF YOU SEE A ROBBERY AT AN APPLE STORE DOES THAT MAKE YOU AN IWITNESS?

WHY DID THE INVISIBLE MAN TURN DOWN THE JOB OFFER?

HE COULDN'T SEE HIMSELF DOING IT.

MY WIFE AND I OFTEN LAUGH ABOUT HOW COMPETITIVE WE ARE.

BUT I DEFINITELY LAUGH MORE.

MY WIFE IS REALLY MAD AT THE FACT THAT I HAVE NO SENSE OF DIRECTION.

SO I PACKED UP MY STUFF AND RIGHT.

MY DRUG TEST CAME BACK. AND IT'S NEGATIVE.

MY DEALER SURE HAS SOME EXPLAINING TO DO.

WHAT DOES A CIA AGENT DO WHEN IT'S TIME FOR BED?

HE GOES UNDER COVER.

WHAT HAPPENED TO THE GUY WHO EMPTIED HIS WALLET INTO A BOWL OF NACHOS?

HE CASHED IN HIS CHIPS.

WHY WAS THE MAN STARING AT THE ORANGE JUICE?

BECAUSE ON THE CONTAINER IT SAID CONCENTRATE.

"DAD, IS IT TRUE YOU GOT SHOT IN THE ARMY?"

"NO, SON. I ONLY GOT SHOT IN THE LEGGY."

WHAT DO YOU CALL A CAN OPENER THAT DOESN'T WORK?

A CAN'T OPENER!

I CAN ONLY HANDLE 25 LETTERS OF THE ALPHABET.

I DON'T KNOW Y.

A CHICKEN COUP ONLY HAS TWO DOORS.

IF IT HAD FOUR, IT WOULD BE A CHICKEN SEDAN.

DAD AT BREAKFAST: "I'LL HAVE BACON AND EGGS, PLEASE."

WAITER: "HOW DO YOU LIKE YOUR EGGS?"

DAD: "I DON'T KNOW, I HAVEN'T GOTTEN THEM YET!"

DAD: "DO YOUR SOCKS HAVE HOLES IN THEM?"

SON: "NO"

DAD: "THEN HOW DO YOU GET YOUR FEET IN THEM?"

WHAT DO ALEXANDER THE GREAT AND WINNIE THE POOH HAVE IN COMMON?

SAME MIDDLE NAME.

MY FRIEND ASKED ME IF I WANTED TO GO TO A MIDDLE EASTERN COUNTRY THAT BORDERS SAUDI ARABIA.

AND I SAID "YEMEN!"

WHAT SHOULD YOU DO IF YOU SEE A SPACE MAN?

PARK IN IT, MAN!

WHAT DID THE BRA SAY TO THE HAT?

"YOU GO ON A HEAD, I GOTTA GIVE THESE TWO A LIFT."

POLICE WERE CALLED TO A DAYCARE CENTER..

WHERE A FOUR-YEAR-OLD WAS RESISTING A REST.

WHAT DO YOU CALL A MILLION RABBITS WALKING BACKWARD?

A RECEDING HARELINE!

WHAT DID THE FISH SAY WHEN IT HIT A CONCRETE WALL?

"DAM!"

"DAD, ARE YOU ALRIGHT?!"

"NO, I'M HALF LEFT."

MOST PEOPLE GET SHOCKED WHEN THEY FIND OUT...

I'M NOT THEIR ELECTRICIAN.

MY NEIGHBOR HAS BEEN MAD AT HIS WIFE FOR SUNBATHING NUDE.

I PERSONALLY AM ON THE FENCE.

I ASKED THE LIBRARIAN IF THEY HAD ANY BOOKS ABOUT PARANOIA.

SHE WHISPERED, "THEY'RE RIGHT BEHIND YOU".

TWO WOMEN WERE SHARING THE SAME ID CARD.

SHARON IS KAREN.

WHILE MOST PUNS MAKE ME NUMB...

MATH PUNS MAKE ME EVEN NUMBER.

DID YOU HEAR ABOUT THE KIDNAPPING AT SCHOOL?

IT'S FINE, HE WOKE UP.

DID YOU HEAR ABOUT THE NEW RESTAURANT ON THE MOON?

GREAT FOOD, NO ATMOSPHERE.

HOW DO YOU MAKE HOLY WATER?

YOU JUST BOIL THE HELL OUT OF IT.

TO THE PERSON WHO STOLE MY COPY OF
MICROSOFT OFFICE,

I WILL FIND YOU. YOU HAVE MY "WORD".

I ACCIDENTALLY GAVE MY WIFE A GLUE STICK
INSTEAD OF A CHAPSTICK.

SHE STILL ISN'T TALKING TO ME.

THE PRESENT, THE PAST, AND THE FUTURE
WALK INTO A BAR...

THINGS GOT A LITTLE TENSE.

WHAT LIES AT THE BOTTOM OF THE SEA AND
TWITCHES?

A NERVOUS WRECK.

MY WIFE TOLD ME TO GET 6 CANS OF SPRITE FROM THE GROCERY STORE.

I REALIZED WHEN I GOT HOME THAT I HAD PICKED 7 UP.

WAITER: "DO YOU WANNA BOX FOR YOUR LEFTOVERS?"

DAD: "NO, I'M MORE OF A WRESTLER."

I TOLD MY FRIEND 10 JOKES TO GET HIM TO LAUGH.

SADLY, NO PUN IN 10 DID.

DID YOU KNOW THE FIRST FRENCH FRIES WEREN'T ACTUALLY COOKED IN FRANCE?

YEAH, THEY WERE COOKED IN GREECE.

I KNOW A LOT OF JOKES ABOUT
UNEMPLOYED PEOPLE...

BUT NONE OF THEM WORK.

I THOUGHT I'D TELL YOU A HILARIOUS
TIME-TRAVEL JOKE,

BUT YOU DIDN'T LIKE IT.

WHAT TRAINING DO YOU NEED TO BECOME A GARBAGE COLLECTOR?

NONE YOU JUST PICK IT UP AS YOU GO ALONG.

DAD, CAN YOU PUT MY SHOES ON?

NO, I DON'T THINK THEY'LL FIT ME.

WHAT DO YOU CALL IT WHEN BATMAN SKIPS CHURCH?

CHRISTIAN BALE.

A BUDDHIST WALKS UP TO A HOTDOG STAND AND SAYS,

"MAKE ME ONE WITH EVERYTHING."

WANT TO HEAR A JOKE ABOUT
CONSTRUCTION? WELL, YOU CAN'T.

I'M STILL WORKING ON IT.

WHERE DOES THE GENERAL KEEP HIS ARMIES?

IN HIS SLEEVIES!

THE SHOVEL WAS A GROUND-BREAKING INVENTION.

THE MATHEMATICIAN WHO INVENTED ZERO?

THANKS A LOT FOR NOTHING.

I WAS FIRED FROM THE BANK ON MY VERY FIRST DAY ON THE JOB.

A WOMAN ASKED ME TO CHECK HER BALANCE, SO I PUSHED HER OVER.

WHAT DO YOU GET WHEN YOU CROSS A DYSLEXIC, AN INSOMNIAC, AND AN AGNOSTIC?

SOMEONE WHO LAYS AWAKE AT NIGHT WONDERING IF THERE IS A DOG.

I'M THINKING ABOUT REMOVING MY SPINE.

I FEEL LIKE IT'S ONLY HOLDING ME BACK.

I WILL NEVER UNDERSTAND WHY MANSLAUGHTER IS ILLEGAL.

MEN SHOULD BE ABLE TO LAUGH AT WHATEVER THEY WANT.

WHY DID THE GHOST SOCCER TEAM WIN ALL THEIR GAMES?

THEY WERE AMAZING AT POSSESSING THE BALL.

WHO LIVES IN A HOUSE WITH ONE BEDROOM, 50 HALLWAYS, AND GHOSTS LURKING EVERYWHERE?

PACMAN

IF CRIMINALS COULD TAKE THEIR OWN MUGSHOTS WHAT WOULD THEY BE CALLED?

CELL-PHIES.

AN INTERESTING FACT ABOUT MOSES:

HE HAD THE FIRST TABLET THAT COULD CONNECT TO THE CLOUD.

WHY DID THE GIRL QUIT HER JOB AT THE DONUT FACTORY?

SHE WAS FED UP WITH THE HOLE BUSINESS.

CAN YOU BELIEVE I GOT FIRED FROM THE CALENDAR FACTORY?

ALL I DID WAS TAKE A DAY OFF.

IF IT'S BAD FOR YOUR HEALTH TO EAT AT NIGHT,

WHY DO THEY PUT A LIGHT IN THE FRIDGE?

I FINALLY DECIDED TO SELL MY VACUUM CLEANER,

BECAUSE ALL IT WAS DOING RECENTLY WAS GATHERING DUST.

CAN FEBRUARY MARCH?

NO, BUT APRIL MAY.

CAN A MATCH BOX?

NO, BUT A TIN CAN!

I WANTED TO MAKE MYSELF A BELT MADE OUT OF WATCHES...

BUT THEN I REALIZED IT WOULD JUST BE A WAIST OF TIME.

I USED TO HATE FACIAL HAIR...

BUT THEN IT GREW ON ME.

WHY WAS KING ARTHUR'S ARMY TOO TIRED TO FIGHT?

BECAUSE IT HAD TOO MANY SLEEPLESS KNIGHTS.

WHAT COUNTRY HAS THE FASTEST-GROWING POPULATION?

IRELAND. BECAUSE EVERY DAY IT'S DUBLIN.

WELL, IF I AGREED WITH YOU...

WE'D BOTH BE WRONG.

HOW DO TREES GET ONLINE?

THEY JUST LOG IN.

WHAT'S THE BEST THING ABOUT LIVING IN SWITZERLAND?

I DON'T KNOW, BUT THEIR FLAG IS A BIG PLUS.

WHEN I DIE I'M DEFINITELY BEING CREMATED.

I'LL HAVE A SMOKING HOT BODY AT LAST.

WHAT IS WORSE THAN ANTS IN YOUR PANTS?

UNCLES!

THE LAST THING I WANT TO DO IS HURT YOU.

BUT HEY, IT'S STILL ON THE LIST.

DID YOU HEAR ABOUT THE SEMI-COLON
THAT BROKE THE LAW?

IT WAS GIVEN TWO CONSECUTIVE SENTENCES.

A DYSLEXIC MAN WALKS INTO A BRA...

I LOST SOME WEIGHT LAST MONTH...

BUT NOW IT FOUND ME AGAIN.

MY CONSCIENCE IS CLEAN.

I HAVEN'T USED IT ONCE UNTIL NOW.

DID YOU HEAR THAT THE WORLD TONGUE-TWISTER CHAMPION GOT ARRESTED?

THEY'RE GONNA GIVE HIM A REALLY TOUGH SENTENCE.

SO WHAT IF I DON'T KNOW WHAT "ARMAGEDDON" MEANS?

IT'S NOT THE END OF THE WORLD.

I DON'T LIKE RUSSIAN DOLLS.

THEY'RE SO FULL OF THEMSELVES.

I LOVE THE WAY THE EARTH SPINS.

IT REALLY MAKES MY DAY.

THE PROBLEM ISN'T THAT OBESITY RUNS IN YOUR FAMILY.

THE ACTUAL PROBLEM IS NO ONE RUNS IN YOUR FAMILY.

I'M ON A SEAFOOD DIET.

EVERY TIME I SEE FOOD, I EAT IT!

THERE ARE THREE TYPES OF PEOPLE:

THOSE WHO CAN COUNT AND THOSE WHO CAN'T.

I ORDERED A CHICKEN AND AN EGG FROM AMAZON.

I'LL LET YOU KNOW.

Made in the USA
Las Vegas, NV
12 December 2022

62022224R00057